Brian ···· ·· lives on the S··· ·· ··· ·· ···· ·· and
two daughters. He writes and edits poetry for young
people. He travels extensively both in the UK and
abroad, presenting his poems in schools and libraries.
He has two poems in *The Nation's
Favourite Children's Poems*.

Other books available from Macmillan

BEWARE

OF THE DINNER LADY!

SCHOOL POEMS
CHOSEN BY BRIAN MOSES

MACMILLAN CHILDREN'S BOOKS

First published 2001 by Macmillan Children's Books as *The School Year*

This edition published 2004 by Macmillan Children's Books
a division of Macmillan Publishers Limited
20 New Wharf Road, London N1 9RR
Basingstoke and Oxford
www.panmacmillan.com

Associated companies throughout the world

ISBN 0 330 43640 6

1 3 5 7 9 8 6 4 2

A CIP catalogue record for this book is available from the British Library.

Printed and bound in Great Britain by
Mackays of Chatham plc, Kent

Contents

Spring Term

Summer Term

Summer Holidays

What Shape is Your Year?

My best friend's year is a long, straight line
That stretches to December.

My teacher's year is an endless loop
From September to September.

But my year is a steep, steep curve
That climbs through winter haze,

Then takes a roller coaster dive
To summer holidays.

Clare Bevan

Autumn Term

Look Out!

The witches mumble horrid chants,
You're scolded by five thousand aunts,
A Martian pulls a fearsome face
And hurls you into Outer Space,
You're tied in front of whistling trains,
A tomahawk has sliced your brains,
The tigers snarl, the giants roar,
You're sat on by a dinosaur.
In vain you're shouting, 'Help' and 'Stop',
The walls are spinning like a top,
The earth is melting in the sun
And all the horror's just begun.
And, oh, the screams, the thumping hearts –
That awful night before school starts.

Max Fatchen

Nine o'Clock Bell!

Nine o'Clock Bell!
Nine o'Clock Bell!
All the small children and big ones as well,
Pulling their socks up, snatching their hats,
Cheeking and grumbling and giving back-chats,
Laughing and quarrelling, dropping their things,
These at a snail's pace, and those upon wings,
Lagging behind a bit, running ahead.
Waiting at corners for lights to turn red,
Some of them scurrying,
Others not worrying,
Carelessly trudging or anxiously hurrying,
All through the streets they are coming pell-mell
At the Nine o'Clock
Nine o'Clock
Nine o'Clock
Bell

Eleanor Farjeon

First Day

I stand at the front in autumn clothes
While children shuffle past in rows.

Who will be mine? The scruffy crowd
Who wriggle and giggle and talk too loud?
The gangly boy with the coconut hair?
The angry child with the angry stare?
The silent girl who stands alone,
Face as blank as a polished stone?
The fidgets, the dreamers, the clumsy crew?
The ones who scratch and the ones who chew?
The ones with eyes rubbed sore and red?
The ones who fill my soul with dread?
Their names are called. Too late to pray.
My fate is sealed. They turn my way.

And the gangly boy who leads the queue
Says, 'All of us hoped we'd be with you.'

Clare Bevan

First Day at School

A millionbillionwillion miles from home.
Waiting for the bell to go. (To go where?)
Why are they all so big, other children?
So noisy? So much at home they
must have been born in uniform.
Lived all their lives in playgrounds
Spent the years inventing games
that don't let me in. Games
that are rough, that swallow you up.

And the railings.
All around, the railings.
Are they to keep out wolves and monsters?
Things that carry off and eat children?
Things you don't take sweets from?
Perhaps they're to stop us getting out.
Running away from the lessins. Lessin.
What does a lessin look like?
Sounds small and slimy.
They keep them in glassrooms.
Whole rooms made out of glass. Imagine.

I wish I could remember my name.
Mummy said it would come in useful.
Like wellies. Then there's puddles.
Yellowwellies. I wish she was here.
I think my name is sewn on somewhere.
Perhaps the teacher will read it for me.
Tea-cher. The one who makes the tea.

Roger McGough

8

It's the First Day Back at School

Brushed and polished, shining,
It's the first day back at school.
Everyone looks different,
Tidy and taller.
Almost like strangers after six weeks.
We line up outside our new classroom,
Jostling to be near the ones we'd like to sit with.
Hoping they will jostle to be near us.
Trying to be first in the line
So that we can choose the best table.
The dreaded Miss Mole appears,
Looking as thin and fierce and frightening
As we were told she was by last year's leavers.
Silence.
We walk in.
Then *rush* to sit where we think we won't be noticed
Or asked questions.
But Miss Mole has a Class Plan
And she moves us all around
To where she can see us.
She asks us *lots* of questions.
The classroom feels alien.
It smells of pine polish and disinfectant
Instead of chalk and damp clothes and sweaty bodies,
Like classrooms should.
And the toilets don't smell at all.
It isn't normal,
It's the first day back at school.
Tomorrow will be better.

Daphne Kitching

New Teacher

She told Henry Baxter off
when he kept fiddling with the velcro
on his new trainers at register time

but Henry Baxter is a pain
and her eyes are soft.

She got all the names wrong
and called Basharat Bash-a-rat
and everyone laughed

but she said sorry
and listened to his name.

She couldn't find
the whiteboard pens and we had
to sit and wait for ages while
she looked in all the drawers and cupboards
then found them on her desk under her big blue bag

but she didn't tell us off
for chatting.

She gave us a poem to read
after break
and I like poems.
It was funny
and even Henry Baxter listened to it.

She remembered my name
when I put my hand up.

And her eyes were soft.

It is early days yet,
but I have high hopes.

Judy Tweddle

Concise Hints for New Teachers

If you get lost on your way to school,
don't ask children for directions.
(They may be dangerous.)

Think twice about wearing the jacket
you imagined was trendy when you were
a student.

Leave Teddy at home.
(Yes, I know he misses you.)

On your first morning, don't confuse
the Head Teacher with the Caretaker.
The Caretaker will never forgive you.

If someone shouts in the corridor,
'Get into line and stop slouching,
you scruffy article,'
they are probably not shouting at you.

It is all right to enter the staffroom without
knocking, and the staff toilet is no longer
out of bounds.

If you confiscate the *Beano* in class
don't be seen swapping it for bubble gum
with the P.E. teacher.

On Open Night, if one of the parent shouts
at you, don't burst into tears.
(Just make a note of the name
and get your own back on the child later.)

Practise scratching your nail down the blackboard –
the kids will hate it.

Bring sandwiches.

Roger McGough

New Boy

He is walking a line: his footsteps mark a square
around the playground. The others forget his name:
a boy that isn't really anywhere.

Wherever he was just then, he isn't there
but somewhere further along, just out of frame.
He is walking a line; his footsteps mark a square

enclosing his teacher, enclosing the autumn air.
She blames no one, knowing she cannot blame
a boy that isn't really anywhere.

He is more than alone. While other children pair
off by the fence and a penalty kicker takes aim,
he is walking a line. His footsteps mark a square

like the edge of a board, a game of solitaire.
He doesn't seem to know another game.
A boy that isn't really anywhere

is on the perimeter. You'd think he doesn't care
about being different. But still, and just the same,
he is walking a line; his footsteps mark a square,
a boy that isn't really anywhere.

Ros Barber

New Shoes

I keep close to walls –
I go the back way –
They made me wear my
Stiff heavy best new
Shoes to school today.

They can't understand it,
I shouldn't be so silly –
But my old ones have got holes in
Or I'd never put these on:
They're just not *me*.

In my desk I sit with them
Tucked under my seat,
These big, bright-boat-size
Brand-new brogues I don't
Want anyone to meet.

– Such as our Miss Wilkins
Who'd look twice and say
As she goes past: 'My, my –
*Some*one's got some nice
New yellow shoes on today.'

I'm hiding in the cloakrooms
(No one's noticed yet),
With my feet under the benches . . .
I *won't* go out,
I'm trying to forget . . .

Like marble pedestals
They fix me to the spot.
Everywhere, I'm caught
In the act of wearing them,
Guilty, though I'm not.

Now I'm standing in the long grass
All on my own.
— I'd sooner have
The Emperor's
New clothes on.

Brian Lee

The Morning Bus

is all of us together every schoolday
piling in with Gary shouting, 'What's the rush?',

is Craig and Jamie racing for the back
and flattening their mugs against the window,

is Susannah showing off her latest project
with its ticks and stars and exclamation marks,

is Michael like an empty lunch-box
in the front seat sitting on his own,

is Megan reading bits from Judy Blume
to Jo who laughs a lot but isn't listening,

is Tony polishing a cloudy marble
held up to the light with one eye closed,

is Craig and Jamie Enterprises' latest plan
for helping us to spend our pocket money,

is Samantha always wearing headphones
unattached to anything except her ears,

is all the reasons we can think of
why Amanda's sitting next to Paul,

is reaching school, and Gary's 'What's the rush?',
and Michael waiting till we've all got off.

John Mole

First Assembly

Teacher says that this morning
we are going to our first
Assembly.
I don't want to go to Assembly.
I didn't like the Tower of London much.
I won't like Assembly.
I have not got my money.
I have not got my packed lunch
or my swimming things . . .
And I don't want to go to Assembly.
I want to stay here in my new school
I like my new school
I like my new teacher
I like my new friends
and the hamster.
> I want to stay here.
> Anyway –
> I can't go to Assembly
> because
> Mum's collecting me after school
> and we are going straight to
> Tescos.

Peter Dixon

Autumn Leaves

Leaves look lost
they flutter and blow around playgrounds
   then sink
      down
         gutters.
Some group into corners
and stay like overnight lodgers!

One or two drift about
as though they are searching for others,
   a lot fall
      from
         the trees
and huddle together
like a soft blanket or cover.

At times the wind
gathers them up and swirls them around,
   like scraps
      of old
         paper
they twirl without sound,
and fall like lost sighs to the ground.

Doris Corti

Tree-Money

Autumn
is tree-money
everywhere on the ground –
red, gold, brown.

Grace Nichols

The Conker Season

Let's get down to the park and smash up a tree,
pull off branches and greenery,
it's the conker season again.

Don't consider the tree or the mess we leave,
throw sticks, throw bricks, give a mighty heave,
it's the conker season again.

Forget all those lessons we did at school
when being green was mega cool.
Don't care what we damage, or break,
when the conker championship's at stake.

Now the only prize is a heavyweight champ
so pull down the fruit, smash and stamp,
it's the conker season again.

And till conker time's past, I know we'll be
environmentally unfriendly,
it's the conker season again.

Brian Moses

Best-of-all Festival

At school the time that's best of all
Is when it's Harvest Festival.
There's fruit and veg and loads of flowers
To be arranged – it all takes hours.
Then we all go in to Assembly –
The hall's jam-packed – it's just like Wembley.
There's mums and dads and teachers there;
The vicar talks and says a prayer;
After the hymns our teacher comes
And lets us chat to dads and mums,
Then it's dinner-time – we've done no sums!

And after lunch, the great display
Is taken down and sent away
To the hospital nearby.
We all help – it makes time fly –
With packing up and making labels
And moving boxes, chairs and tables.
There's just no time to write or spell –
It's end of school, there goes the bell.

Oh yes, the best school day of all
Is when it's Harvest Festival.

Eric Finney

A Harvest Prayer

'And now, children, let us thank
God for all the good things
He has given us . . .'

Thank you, Lord, for what we eat,
For fields of corn, and rice, and wheat;
Thank you for the fruits of toil
That we bring forth from your good soil.
Thank you, Lord . . . for hot, crisp fries,
And burgers of enormous size;
Thank you, Lord, for chocolate shakes,
And all those lovely, sticky cakes;
Thank you for large cans of Coke,
And Mr Williams, who tells jokes,
And never makes us do revision.
Thank you, Lord, for television,
For quizzes, soaps and films that thrill;
Please, Lord, make them scarier still!
Thank you for my mountain bike,
For giving me some friends to like;
For comics, trainers, videos, pop –
Oh let those sweet sounds never stop!
Thank you for computer games,
And helping me avoid the blame
When someone set the hamster free,
Although I swear it wasn't me.
Thank you, Lord, for Christmas Day,
For playtimes and for holidays,

For bubble gum . . . such wondrous things!
And hear my voice now, as I sing
To thank thee once, and once again,
For thy great bounty, Lord . . . Amen!

Tony Bradman

Photo Opportunity

I'm waiting in line
For the class photo
I'm getting my face ready
Trying out
A few expressions
A few good looks:
casual
hard
INTERESTING
cool
I think I'll go
for *casual*-***cool***
And wait for the shutter to click.
Clunk!

So
How come
When the photos come back
In their special offer pack
I look just like I did
(Just another soppy kid)
Last time?

Trevor Millum

School Photo Day

Here's a tale of Meryl Rose
Who liked to push things up her nose . . .
    Lego, biscuits
        Beads and bread –
            Rattled round inside her head.

A foolish girl – who wasted days
Playing with her silly craze –

    Until upon school photo day
    She got the hamster out to play,
    And with a grin and Meryl pout
    She pushed poor Hammy up her snout!

'Look this way,' called photo man
'Smile or giggle if you can . . .'

Sweet Meryl posed
      with smile
        and pout –

And half a hamster hanging out!

Peter Dixon

Half-Term

One day to start on your homework,
One day to mess around,
One day to tidy your bedroom,
One day to shop in town.
One day to be baked by the sunshine,
One day to be soaked by the wet.
One day to visit the dentist,
The hairdresser and the vet.
One day to finish that homework,
One day to see your friend –
Half-term's hardly started,
Before it's come to an end.

Penny Dolan

Shopping List for a Firework Display

One sharp, frosty night.
An inky-black midnight sky.
Several metres of safety barrier.
A circle of Catherine Wheels.
A bouquet of Crick-Crack Chrysanthemums.
A hoppit of Jumping Jacks.
A cacophony of Crackling Thunderbursts.
A zoom of Flight Rockets.
A cloudburst of Golden Showers.
A brilliance of Roman Candles.
A boom of Quadblast Bangers.
A zigzag of Sing Birds.
A torrent of Silver Fountains.
A rainbow of Bursting Violets.
One match.
15 minutes of magic.
One million Oohs and Aahs.

Irene Yates

Our School's Firework Night

We exploded into the playground
Fizzing with excitement,
Spinning and crackling with laughter,
Twirling our torches to write our names
On the November air.

Little brothers stood at the front,
Bundled and muffled in zipped warmth.
Little sisters spiralled like smoke
Around their mothers' skirts.

The countdown began.

Across the field we saw the first spark
Dart down to touch the poised row of rockets.
We held our ears
Dreading and longing for
The Big Scream.

And the rain started.
Gentle for a while,
Spitting, teasing, frizzing our hair,
Staining our shoulders
Until the babies began to wail.
Then faster and harder,
Soaking our shoes,
Sending cold streams of misery
Down our collars,
Down our upturned faces.

The crowd bloomed with umbrellas
As the far-off fathers ran with smouldering fuses
To light the lovely displays.
Catherine Wheels that twisted off their sticks,
Fiery Flowers that wilted and drooped
Against the gloomy sky,
Mighty Atoms that popped like paper bags,
Volcano Mountains that erupted with choking green fog,
And a final, forlorn message
To send us home.
' _ _OD _IG _ _.'

'Good night,' we called sadly
As we trailed away
Like damp squibs.
'Od ig.
Od ig.'

Clare Bevan

Remembrance

Sometime around Remembrance Day
Our grans came into school
To tell us what they could remember.
'Visits to the sweetshop with the ration book.'
'Listen With Mother on the radio.'
'Spiders in the outside toilet!'
'Photos of young men in uniform.'
'Buying a television for the coronation.'
'Teachers who threw chalk and blackboard rubbers!'
'Crinkly nylon bathing costumes. Holidays in Blackpool.'
'Gramophones you wound up with a handle!'
'Groceries delivered in a van.'
They made us smile, our grans.
'Ah, yes,' they said, 'life was much simpler then.'
We made them coffee, then they took
Their treasured memories home again.

Sue Cowling

We Will Remember Some of Them

Every year they sell poppies at our school.
Someone goes round all the classes with a tray.
Single poppies
Double poppies
Sprays of poppies,
Huge poppies for cars,
And, best of all poppies, on wooden crosses.
Like swords.
No one's allowed to buy those
Because one year Peter Potts got two for a pound
And fought a duel with Billy Watson.
Our head said it was disrespectful
And banned them.

They're to remind us of the wars
And the men who died.
They do it every year so that we'll never forget
The eleventh hour of
The eleventh day of
The eleventh month,
When the fighting stopped,
But the crying and the dying didn't.

My great-grandad was in
The Second World War.
He was a footballer before he had to go.
He didn't want to be a soldier.
He didn't want to go, but he had to.
Had to leave his wife, his baby and the team.
He was too old to play when the war ended,

So he sold bread and never had holidays.

He came back.
He would have been eighty-three next birthday,
But last November was cold.
His fire was turned right down when
He died.
And every year they sell poppies . . .

Daphne Kitching

Remembrance Day Remembered

For the sake of men we never knew
We trooped into the hall
Where their names in golden letters
Were written on the wall.

Somebody sounded a bugle
And ghosts seemed everywhere
Until the last note softly fell
On the suddenly empty air.

Then the world filled up with living
In its own accustomed way,
With the usual busy traffic
Of the usual busy day.

But what I most remember
And know that I always will
Is how we stood utterly silent
And absolutely still.

John Mole

Playtime in Autumn

It's playtime and a pale mist swirls
dampening clothes and straightening curls
leaving diamond drops of dew
on trees and plants and noses too.
It blocks large buildings out of sight
to make an eerie world of white
where birds sit silent, feathers ruffled.
Every sound is soft and muffled.
Children clump in little crowds.
They feel as if they're in a cloud,
then dwindle, wraith-like, faint and grey,
swallowed by the foggy day.
Their teacher shivers, cold and wet.
Isn't playtime over yet?
'Come in,' she cries and rings the bell
and children scamper up, pell-mell
and tramp inside with clomping feet
to where there's colour, noise and heat.

Marian Swinger

Wet Day

It's rained every day now
Every day for a week.

The bus splashes to a halt and the queue piles on.
Hats off,
Hoods down,
Coats drip, drip.

The world through the window,
Wiped by a dozen hands and hats and gloves,
Is an out of focus rush.

I count the stops to school.

The classroom smells of steam coats,
Sodden socks and puddle-drenched shoes.
Thirty boys sit too close together
At desks they have outgrown.

Just as they begin to feel
Warmth return to their toes,
They are sent out into the playground again.
To seek shelter in the sheds.

Where sullenly they watch
As eager-faced footballers
Whoop in wild delight.

It's rained every day now,
Every day for a week.

I think it's going to rain for ever.

Colin McEwan

Banned

Mud's good
But it's banned.
Because we tread in it, and then we tread it in.

The field's good.
But it's banned.
We're not allowed out on the field unless it's dry,
Which it never is.

Snow's good.
But it's banned.
Because it melts and goes to slush
And then the dirt and slush gets mushed
And makes mud.

Mud's good.
But it's banned.

Jan Dean

I Went Back

I went back after a cold
And nothing was the same.
When the register was called
Even my name
Sounded queer . . . new . . .
(And I was born here too!)
Everyone knew more than me,
Even Kenneth Hannaky
Who's worst usually.
They'd made a play
And puppets from clay
While I was away,
Learnt a song about Cape Horn,
Five guinea pigs were born.
Daffodils in the blue pot,
(I planted them)
Bloomed, and I was not
There to see.
Jean had a new coat
And someone, probably George,
Smashed my paper boat.
Monday was a dreadful day.
I wished I was still away.
Tuesday's news day.
I took my stamps to show,
Made a clown called Jo,
Learnt that song from John . . .

Cold's almost gone . . .
And . . . the smallest guinea pig,
Silky black and brown thing,
I'm having
Till spring.

Gwen Dunn

Grey Squirrel

Noses against the classroom windows,
teacher standing behind us, we stare out
as a grey squirrel nimbles its way
over the field's million sodden leaves
on this damp November day.

The trees drip, the grass is dank,
the playground shines like plastic.
A bedraggled sun. All's still, still,
except for that squirrel now busy
at husks of beech nuts, nibbling his fill.

Suddenly he's bolt upright, sniffing,
and then gone, swarming up a tree trunk
like Spiderman scaling a vertical wall.
Now he tight-rope-runs along a branch
and leaps to the next tree, does not fall.

We return to our tables. Chairs scrape.
Teacher stands at the board, chalk poised.
No one speaks. For a minute we secretly gloat
over the wonder of that squirrel
in leather gloves and grey fur coat.

Wes Magee

Diwali

In our house
the lamps are lit,
sweetmeats set out for friends to eat.

Diwali! Diwali!
Festival of lights.

In our town
the roads are closed,
no buses, lorries, cars allowed.

A friendly crowd walks up,
strolls down.
The Golden Mile a promenade.

Strangers smile,
faces bright . . .
everywhere is strung with lights.

We all feel great,
laugh and shake hands.
Namaste and gifts exchanged.

People sharing,
families meet:
talking, greeting, celebrate

Diwali! Diwali!
Festival of lights.

Joan Poulson

Prince Rama Comes to Longsight

A hundred points of flame
Fleet and weave upon their wicks
On a wet Manchester morning;
But the hall curtains are closed
Against the littered streets,
And incense burns
In a blob of Plasticine
On every window ledge.

The children are changed;
An exotic orient breath
Has lifted their spirits.
No longer poor and grubby kids
From the wrong side of town:
Sayed, from class three,
Is now Prince Rama,
Splendid in his cardboard crown,
With Nilam-Sita
Trembling by his side,
And Hanuman, the monkey-king,
Fit to burst with monkey-pride.

Will they forget their words?
Will the infants wail?
At first sight of the monster
And its glittering teeth?
No matter.
The legend holds us in its spell,
As in a perfumed bubble,
Lit by lapping flames.

The story moves to its close,
And Miss asks little David
To please stop picking his nose.
She thanks us for our work
And says that next week,
Class Four will give
A Chinese assembly.

The candles are snuffed,
Leaving a greasy smell
To mingle with the boiling cabbage.
Sir nips the incense out.
We are back in rainy Manchester,
But we are not the same.
Though Sayed is himself again.

Puzzling over
Rainbow Maths – Book Three.
And Nilam-Sita has been sent
To fetch a teacher's cup of tea;
Something of Prince Rama
Stays with us;
Sita's beauty,
Hanuman's guile;
Some touch of splendour
From a fabled land.

John Cunliffe

Eight Candles Burning

Three stars in the sky;
the children have counted them twice.
The menorah is polished,
the matches to hand,
ready to set a candle alight,
today, tomorrow and every night
until we see
          eight candles burning.

Bright as the stars,
the children's eyes and promises.
Parents, grandparents are children again,
thankful for freedom,
happy to see a candle light,
today, tomorrow and every night
until we see
          eight candles burning.

Around the table
faces are glowing at stories retold.
Like the flame of the match
hearts are burning,
eager to set a candle alight,
today, tomorrow and every night
until we see
          eight candles burning.

Celia Warren

School Play

I missed out on the school play
they always miss out me
I hoped to be a soldier
a pirate or a tree . . .
   but no one ever chose me
   and I didn't get a part
   so I'm helping with the curtains
   and putting out the chairs.
I'm stacking all the tables
I'm sorting out the ropes
saying when we're ready
and hanging up the coats.
I'm first reserve for peasant
and third for chorus line
helping Mrs Watson
and handing out the wine.
But I'd rather be a soldier
and I'd really like to sing
but boys like me stack tables
and boys like me aren't kings.

Peter Dixon

Just Doing My Job

I'm one of Herod's Henchmen.
We don't have much to say,
We just charge through the audience
In a Henchman sort of way.

We all wear woolly helmets
To hide our hair and ears,
And Wellingtons sprayed silver
To match our tinfoil spears.

Our swords are made of cardboard
So blood will not be spilled
If we trip and stab a parent
When the hall's completely filled.

We don't look very scary,
We're mostly small and shy,
And some of us wear glasses,
But we give the thing a try.

We whisper Henchman noises
While Herod hunts for strangers,
And then we all charge out again
Like nervous Power Rangers.

Yet when the play is over
And Miss is out of breath
We'll charge like Henchmen through the hall
And scare our mums to death.

Clare Bevan

Pantomime Poem

I'm going to write a pantomime poem
OH NO YOU'RE NOT!
Oh yes I am!
One that will get everyone going
OH NO YOU'RE NOT!
Oh yes I am!

There'll be huge custard pies
And girls who slap thighs,
Men dressed in frocks
And bloomers with dots,
There'll be beanstalks and castles,
Some heroes, some rascals.
There'll be goodies to sing to
And villains BEHIND YOU!
There'll be eggs that are golden,
An actor who's an old 'un!
Cows all called Daisy
And songs that are crazy!

I'm going to write a pantomime poem
OH NO YOU'RE NOT!
Oh yes I am!
One that will get everyone going
OH NO YOU'RE NOT!
Oh yes I am!
OH NO YOU'RE NOT!
Oh yes I am!
OH NO YOU'RE NOT!
I just did!

Coral Rumble

Disco Night

In the girls' cloakroom
the air gasps with *Nightfall* and *Moonwind*.
    The excitement is intense.
Everyone uses the
strawberry-flavoured lip gloss
    passed round by Geraldine Spence.

In a giggling gaggle the girls
rush to the school hall
    where the floor shines like a skating rink.
Loud music throbs and pounds.
The disco lights dazzle with flashes of
    red, mauve, yellow, green and pink.

And *he's* there, Dean Moffat
in a big stripy shirt
    and with gel on his spiky hair.
When the deejay yells,
'*Go grab 'em, girls!*'
    Lisa drags him, protesting, off his chair.

* * * * * * * *

Next morning, Lisa is at the centre
of a playground huddle of girls.
    '*What happened?*' '*Tell us!*' '*Own up!*'
Lisa smiles. '*I think he loves me,*'
she says, '*and I bet he marries me
    when we're grown up!*'

Wes Magee

A Week to Christmas

Sunday with six whole days to go.
How we'll endure it I don't know!

Monday the goodies are in the making
Spice smells of pudding and mince pies a-baking.

Tuesday, Dad's home late and quiet as a mouse
He smuggles packages into the house.

Wednesday's the day for decorating the tree,
Will the lights work again? We'll have to see!

Thursday's for last-minute shopping and hurry,
We've never seen Mum in quite such a flurry!

Friday is Christmas Eve when we'll lie awake
Trying to sleep before the daybreak

And that special quiet of Christmas morn
When out there somewhere Christ was born.

John Cotton

Winter Term

Headmasters and headmistresses
Have chopped the year in three:
We've autumn, spring and summer terms,
But where can winter be?

What have they done with winter? Do
They think they're being kind
In making us feel winter is
A figment of the mind?

It seems that winter's been condensed
To just two weeks or three,
Renamed the Christmas holiday –
That's how it seems to me.

Colin West

Spring Term

Ten New Year's Resolutions

To do my homework every night   if there's no match on TV
To be nice to Miss Tomkins   ugh!
To visit Gran   on her baking day
To save some pocket money   to spend on ice cream
To bring my sports kit back
    for Mum to wash   before it walks home
To tidy my room   ~~at weekends~~ occasionally
To go to bed on time   with a torch
To eat at least *one* green vegetable   a pea
To improve my maths   a fraction
To scrap these resolutions   without hesitation

Mina Johnson

Day Closure

We had a day closure on Monday
and I spent the morning in bed,
but the teachers went in as usual
and someone taught them instead.

And I thought of them all in the classroom,
stuck to their seats in rows,
some of them sucking pen lids.
Head Teacher scratching his nose.

Perhaps it's a bit like an M.O.T.
to check if teachers still know
the dates of our kings and queens
or the capital of so and so.

Perhaps they had tables and spellings,
did the Head give them marks out of ten?
And then, if they got any wrong,
did he make them learn them again?

I thought of them out at break time
playing football or kiss chase or tag,
picking up teams in the playground
or scoffing crisps from a bag.

If I'd been a fly on the wall,
I might have watched while they slaved,
I'd have seen who asked silly questions
Or if anyone misbehaved.

I thought of them all going home,
crossing the road to their mums.
They looked very grim the next day.
It couldn't have been much fun.

Brian Moses

Winter Playground

In the cold winter sunshine
The children stand against the wall.
They look like washing on a line,

Neat red coat, stripy mitts,
Narrow green tights with a hole in the knee.
Still and stiff, frozen in a row.

Across the playground
Three boys are chasing a ball.
A little dog barks through the fence.

A skipping rope curves –
'One I love, two I loathe . . . ' –
As the girls hop and jump.

The teacher stalks, eyes darting,
Scattering marbles in his way,
Keeping a lookout for TROUBLE.

But from the train window
It's the still ones I see, the quiet ones,
Straight and stiff against the wall,
Like washing, frozen on the line.

Jennifer Curry

Cold Day – Edinburgh

Before my eyes open,
I smell the crisp, clean, cold air.

Windows splashed with ferns of frost.
Too cold to wash,
Just straight into clothes,
Then downstairs to big bowls of porridge.

In the street the roofs and cars and trees
Are sugar-coated.
We stand and stamp our feet
As steaming kettles pour over
Frozen locks and windscreens.
Exhaust clouds boil
And mingle with the smell of the brewery.

We are driven slowly to school.

Grim-faced salt-wielding janitors
Destroy lethal slides
As we sit huddled over Bunsen burners in the lab.
Then the note from the Office arrives –
'The boiler can't take it,
The school is too cold.'

So we go home to frozen pipes
And hot chocolate,
To wrap up in travelling rugs,
Sit on the storage heater,
And watch *South Pacific* on the telly.

Colin McEwan

Supply Teacher

Here is the rule for what to do
Whenever your teacher has the flu,
Or for some other reason takes to her bed
And a different teacher comes instead.

When this visiting teacher hangs up her hat,
Writes the date on the board, does this or that;
Always remember, you must say this:
'*Our* teacher never does that, Miss!'

When you want to change places or wander about,
Or feel like getting the guinea pig out,
Never forget, the message is this:
'*Our* teacher always lets us, Miss!'

Then, when your teacher returns next day
And complains about the paint or clay,
Remember these words, you just say this:
'That *other* teacher told us to, Miss!'

Allan Ahlberg

In Winter

In winter we stamp in the playground
   and run
Make slides on the ice, crack puddles
   for fun.
In winter our breath puffs out
   cloudy white.
Blue smoke drifts up in the pale
   soft light.
In winter night comes early,
   comes soon;
Frost in the air and a high
   cold moon.
Walking home at dusk we see
   windows glow
Making yellow pools on the new
   fallen snow.

Penny Kent

Snow Memory

(for Bridget)

We'd never seen snow like it;
thick on pavements, drifting up walls.

That morning Mr Jones, the Head,
called everyone into the hall.
'Before you get too excited,' he drawled,
'let's remember some safety rules:
no slides, no snowballs, no icicle swords
and, if it's snowing hard at lunchtime,
everyone stays indoors.'

We all groaned.
'Don't worry,' he joked.
'The snow will still be there
when you get home.'

All morning we tried to work
but grey skies and curtains of flakes
big as white Walkers crisps
drew our eyes to each window space.
Lunchtime – still snowing, of course!
Then the afternoon bell.
The snow stopped
and we mumbled and cursed.

Last lesson was double games.
What a hope! Indoor rounders, at best!
'Come along,' said Miss Prest.
'Get your coats, boots and wellies.
Gloves on – follow me.'
Through the deep snow we stomped
and on to the sports field.
'Right,' she said, 'into teams of four.
Marks out of ten for the best
snow creatures you can build.
See what you score.'

It was ten times more sweat,
ten times more work
than for any games lesson
– but ten times more fun!
We shaped squirrels, rabbits, a lion,
crocodile, cat, kangaroo . . .
laughing, we filled the field
with a whole snow zoo.

When we'd finished,
we all stood and cheered
(including Miss Prest)
but the stunned, amazed look
on Mr Jones' face was the best.

One magical day
none of us ever forgot;
one about which we still talk
whenever we see
snow fall.

Patricia Leighton

Slide Time Sonnet
(A Sonnet)

The slide's become a sheet of greasy glass
As queues of children glide wide-eyed across
The chilly yard. Class after eager class
Soon joins the cheerful lines upon the gloss
That boots and shoes have made of playground ice.
Each teacher sees this fun with nervous smile,
And wishes she could also skate this paradise
With all her childhood skating grace and style.
And then a wobbling stumble, trip and fall.
A growing mound of bodies quickly grows,
A crawling, sprawling, brawling caterwaul.
Is that a fractured arm? A broken nose?
The Head appears with pails of salty sand.
The slide soon melts. So does the skating band.

John Kitching

Netball

When
trying
to score
at netball
it helps
if you're
more
than
usually
normally
excess-
ively
extra-
ordinar-
ily
tall.

Ann Bonner

When I Think

When I think of all the games I could have played,
All the skills I could have learned –
Racing incredibly fast cars
Round improbable bends;
Skating at dawn on frozen lakes
Where I carve cobwebs with my sizzling blades;
Scuba-diving through a forest of coral
To feed blue lobsters and friendly sea horses by hand;
Defying glaciers and avalanches
To plant my flag on Everest's silver crown,
Then skiing back through the marshmallow snow;
Shooting the rapids in a skin-tight kayak;
Fencing like a female musketeer;
Vaulting as high as the startled sparrows;
Swatting feathered shuttlecocks with my swift racquet;
Leaping over treacherous water jumps
And leading my steaming stallion into the winner's
enclosure;
Outclassing the whole field at polo;
Snookering Steve Davis;
Out-running Flo Jo;
Knocking out Bruno;
Jousting and judo . . .

There must be a thousand sports I could have sampled.

So why should it be
That I'm here again,
Losing a netball match
In the pouring rain?

Clare Bevan

67

The Last Laugh

Jacko floated over the corner
less than a minute, the score two-all
in our under-elevens cup-final.
I leapt like a salmon up a waterfall
high above the defence, meeting
the ball with a perfect header until
an elbow sharp as a bayonet
stuck into my side and cut out my breath.
I fell to the grass like a burst balloon
face down in the mud, the air knocked from me.
The ball, a useless, harmless bubble,
floated past the post towards the corner.
Their full-back's face, like a monster mask,
grinned as I slipped and slurped in the dirt.
He held out his arm to help me get up
then pushed me back over, whispering,
Got you that time, didn't I, mate,
thought you'd won? That'll teach you!
He straightened up, laughed again
when he heard the whistle he knew was full time.
But I saw the ref standing just behind him.
That whistle meant I was going to score
the match-winning goal from the penalty spot.

David Harmer

February 14th

I like that boy
in Mrs Jones's class.
I like his face.

He doesn't know
me, although
when we
were in the playground
I thought he
looked at me.
Once.

I could give him
some secret
sign. I know his
address. He'd
never guess
who sent
a Valentine.

Ann Bonner

Valentine's Day

Valentine's Day can be hard if you don't receive a card
so this year I've got it fixed – I have posted myself six.
What's this? The postman has brought seven!
A real card! Wow! I'm in heaven.
Wait a minute, I'm not dumb
this card was written by
my mum. Oh well.
I can truly say
I am loved on
Valentine's
Day.

Jane Clarke

We're Book Weak

Authors we've never heard of
Are coming to our school
To tell us how they 'write' their books –
So we'll just 'play it cool'
And smile at them politely
And try hard NOT to doze
Or start a fit of coughing
Or sniff and pick our nose.
They may be pretty boring
(They might read lots of VERSE!)
But at least we're MISSING science and maths,
So you see it COULD be worse ... !

Trevor Harvey

Tuup the Story-Teller

He counted us on his African drum,
the story began, CRICK-CRACK.
A fish swam out of his moving hands,

a crow flew out of his mouth.
His fingernails were razor talons,
his skull an eagle's head.

He rose from the sea
to look at the view,
he grew and grew and grew.

He made a sound
like a whistling sigh,
I know what he was, do you?

Chrissie Gittins

School Visit

The Great Merlanda's here today
with tricks and traps and spells;
there's not a murmur in the hall,
you'd hear a speck of stardust fall
except
      for Jim
         who
fidgets, fiddles,
whispers, wriggles,
sniggers, giggles,
won't sit still
     till
        at last

The Great Merlanda,
footsteps ringing,
cloak a-swinging,
strides right down
past seated pupils
reaches Jim's row,
simply yells . . .

IF YOU DON'T SIT IN YOUR CHAIR, BOY,

I'll . . .

turn you into a rabbit
and stuff you in my hat,
I'll lock you up in my bottomless box
or places worse than that!
I'll turn you into the six of spades
and deal you out to the Head;
I'll saw you in two then tie up the bits
in a granny-knot, I said!
I'll turn you into a handkerchief
or a mouse to play with my cat!
If you can't sit still
      RIGHT NOW
         on that chair . . .

Said Jim,
      'I'll do just that!' ·

            Judith Nicholls

Recyclable 'Thank You' Letter for School Visitors

Simply underline the words that you need

Dear –
Poet
Pet Shop Owner
Librarian
Traffic Warden

Thank you ever so much for visiting our school –
Yesterday
Last week
Last term (whooops!!).

We all thought you were –
Quite
Surprisingly
Extremely

Interesting
Different

Your –
Nature poems
Stick insects and lizard
Gardening books
Lollipop

were –
Unusual

Quite funny
Unforgettable
Different

and are still –
Talked about in the staffroom
Crawling about in the staffroom cupboard

We haven't –
Laughed as much
Had such a fascinating day –

Since
Ever

We're very sorry about –
. . . 's rude question
The school dinner
The class hamster
. . . showing you her unrivalled collection of rubbers

– let's hope it won't happen next time.

Once again, thank you very much for the visit, it –
'Was very educational'(said Miss)
'Gave an invaluable insight into your work' (said the
Head Teacher)
Meant we missed numeracy AND literacy hours!

Yours sincerely

James Carter

Tadpoles

For J.W.

Since my first infant term I remember
their surprise arrivals brought a pleasure
keen and not predicted by the calendar.

One morning you would see glass glint, feel squirms
of fascination rippling into grins.
Our teachers took down old aquariums

from cupboard tops. We rinsed them clean of dust
then filled them with sieved pond-water at first.
After that for topping up the tap sufficed.

One overflowing year Mike Cotton came
with an enamel bucket brimming spawn –
too much for classroom conservation.

Everybody took a handful
in lunchbox, jar or milkbottle.
My plastic bag leaked a trickle

of sticky seepage that ran down
my legs and prompted curious frowns
on faces on the bus back home.

They hatched and grew fat on the windowsill
safe in a flower-vase untouched until
(come round to help a bit) my Aunty Jill

poured them accidentally down the toilet,
then said the family must have something desperate.
My mother never quite forgave her that.

Philip Tupper fed them one by one
to his piranha. Lizzie kept hers in
a bowl until her puppy drank them. When

Jemma's died she pressed them all like leaves
between the pages of a book. Now these
dippings into childhood pools draw symphonies

into a single jar intense and bright
with remembered water, sky and weed and light:
the crotchets quivering their silent music.

Barrie Wade

Eid Mela

'This week,' said our teacher,
'We are going to study Eid Mela.'
But she told us all she knew
In five minutes flat,
And we couldn't draw Mecca.
'So let's try something traditional,'
She said.
'Let's all paint our hands instead.'

Sunil and I sat elbow to elbow,
Fighting as usual.
We were the last to start
And the last to finish.
I decorated my broad left palm
With a crowd of smiley faces
In red and green and blue.
Sunil, very carefully,
Covered his slim left palm
With a delicate cobweb
Of sunshine-coloured strands.

At playtime, we argued,
Pushed out our hands
Pressed like wrestlers
Until we crumpled on the warm tarmac.

Then we looked at our sticky skin.

Sunil's warm right palm
Held a smudged rainbow of smiles.

My damp right palm
Was strung with golden threads.
And we began to laugh.
'Happy Eid Mela,' we giggled,
Waving our mirror hands in the air.
'Happy Eid.
Partner.'

Clare Bevan

Windy Playground

They played blow-me-down in the yard,
letting the wind bully them,
coats above heads, arms spread wide,
daring the wind to do its worst.
They leant forward against the blow
as it rallied and flung them back,
then coats puffed out like clouds
they returned to attack the blast,
while the gale drew a breath and then
pressed relentless. Till wild in defeat
and magnificent, they grouped again
and stretched their wings, stubborn
as early airmen.

Brian Moses

Mother's Day

Out the cupboard
here it comes,
lots of card
for all our mums,
for it's that time,
nearly Mother's Day,
when we stick
our way through play.

We love to cut,
it's so much fun,
we'd happily make cards
for everyone,
so how about
we start a craze,
let's not just have
Mother's Days!

But brothers, sisters,
uncles too,
nephews, nieces
to name but few,
doctors, nurses
and the rest,
then, at school,
we'd try our best.

For making cards
is our real skill
anything else
is all downhill,
it's every subject
into one,
so let's make cards,
for everyone!

Andrew Collett

Mother's Day Prayer

Dear God
Today is Mother's Day.
Please make her backache go away.

May her pot plants all grow healthy
and a lottery win make her wealthy.

May our dad buy her some flowers
and take us all to Alton Towers.

May her fruitcake always rise
and the sun shine bright
in her blue skies.

Roger Stevens

April 1st

Our teacher's looking nervous,
I think she's feeling tense –
sixty eyes all watch her closely,
we're tingling with suspense.
She shrewdly tests her chair seat,
before daring to sit down –
her eyes flick, spy-like, round the room
under a worried frown.
She peers into her pencil pot
as if it's going to bite –
and slowly takes her pencil out
to check before she writes.
Our thirty watchful faces
all tell that something's up –
then her attention fastens
on her waiting coffee cup.
'I think I'll leave my coffee,
till after registration,
I apologize if this frustrates
your keen anticipation!'
She opens up the register,
says, 'It's very quiet in school . . . '
then out it jumps, and she screams, 'AAAARGH!'
and we scream, 'APRIL FOOL!'

Liz Brownlee

April Fool

Imran thought of it,
Jack said, *Go on,*
Kim said, *Yeah,*
But I did it.

Imran said, *Cool,*
Jack said, *Stupendous,*
Kim said, *My hero,*
Our class went ballistic.

Sir picked himself up,
Breathed slowly and deeply
For what seemed like ages,
Then pointed his finger.

All afternoon while the rest
Are at swimming
I'm scrubbing graffiti.
It's not fair, it's slave labour.

I've said it before
On many occasions
The trouble with teachers is
No sense of humour.

Frances Nagle

Rain

Rain.
I had to be Rain.
For the Easter pageant.
Picked from the whole class!
'Picked from the whole school!' my teacher said
To Grandad,
Who grasped my hand, shook it firmly,
And mouthed, 'Well done, son!'
While Tim and Lee and Dean and Mike
Smirked,
And my sister
Gave me the sign for endless teasing.
Rain.
How my heart sank.
Sleepless nights,
Rings beneath my eyes,
Bitten nails,
And endless, endless teasing.
Until
There I stood
That Friday morning,
Dull as ditch-water,
Next to Storm showing off
In billowing cloak,
With cymbal-clashing Thunderbolt,
And Sun and Moon and Easter Egg like beauty queens,
And Ocean, Stream and Tree in flowery green,
And me
In grey dungarees,
Holding a watering can.

Me, standing there on Mr Preedy's cart,
My teacher calling,
'Perfect, perfect, Daniel!
You look just the part.'

Mary Green

Easter in School

We've practised all the Easter hymns
And brought in eggs to boil.
We've made them into 'egg heads'
(Mine's a Martian dressed in foil)

We've all made tissue daffodils
To take home to our mums,
Baked Easter Bunny biscuits
(And licked up all the crumbs!)

It's Friday, end-of-term at last!
We're busy making cards.
We're using best art paper
And I'm sharing mine with Harj.

I've pasted on bright flowers, a chick,
A golden sun above,
A glitter **Happy Easter**
And inside *With lots of love.*

I sneak a look at Harj's card.
'Hey, Harj, what's that big splosh?'
'That's the green hill far away,' she says.
'And that's the cross.'

Patricia Leighton

Easter

The year turns at Easter time.

Button buds collect on the branches
and like a sprinkling of young yellow suns,
bright daffodils colour
the hibernating fields and hedgerows.

The year turns, slowly and silently, into spring
and everywhere the newborn chicks, lambs and fledglings
struggle to be seen, heard and noticed.
Out of the grey, bare days of weak winter
the sacred strength of spring emerges.

The year turns and Mother Earth lifts her ashen face
to the pale blue of the brightening sky.
In celebration she pushes up
the timeclocks of the ages –
a flourish of flowers, a blast of blossom.

John Rice

Summer Term

The Test

I'm not looking forward to tomorrow,
For tomorrow we've got the Test.
Mum's told me to try not to worry
And just to do my best.

But I can't get to sleep for wondering
What the questions will be,
And what if my friends all pass and go
To a different school from me.

It's no good pretending I'll ever
Come out top of the class.
I only hope that I get enough marks
To be one of the few who pass.

John Foster

Exams

Exams aren't fun.
You don't get many people
going to exams for their holidays.

They don't show exam highlights
on Match of the Day,
there's no Exam of the Month competition
or action replays.

You can't chew or drink exams
and when you put them on
they're really dull and dated.

No, exams aren't cheerful.
Imagine taking an exam to the disco,
who'd do that?

Or paying to see one dance and sing
at an end-of-the-pier show?

You'd think my teachers
would agree with me, see
the reason in what I'm saying.

If exams had been here years ago
they'd all have been hanged
for sleep-stealing.

David Harmer

Inside ... Out

Inside it's tests today.
Are seven eights fifty-six
or sixty-four?
How many degrees
in a triangle and –
what *is* a hypotenuse?

> *Outside two magpies*
> *strut the tarmac,*
> *jumping into the wind.*
> *Zoom up to the very*
> *top of the conifers.*
> *Wish I was them.*

Thirty minutes to write
a *really* exciting story
Miss said.
Twenty minutes, it's done;
everyone captured or
dead except me.

> *Outside on the grass*
> *a gang of dry leaves,*
> *light as air,*
> *plays a wild game*
> *of ring-o'-roses.*
> *Wish I was there.*

'Design a boat
to carry six marbles,'
the DT paper said.
'Construct it and test.
Does it float?'
Does it heck!

> *Year Fives are at games,*
> *girls on the rounders pitch,*
> *boys on Top Field;*
> *wind tugging shirts,*
> *cheeks bright red.*
> *Wish I could join in.*

Next, World War Two.
Black-outs and Spitfires
– fill in this map –
list a week's rations and –
what *does* a doodlebug do?

> *Through the top window*
> *tumbling clouds run*
> *relays across the sky,*
> *heading for new horizons,*
> *racing free . . .*
> *wish it was me.*

> *Patricia Leighton*

Yesterday it Happened

After weeks of widths and armbands,
After a lifetime of 'Long legs' and floats,
After terms and terms of trying so hard,
And gallons of pool up my nose,
Yesterday it happened.

I pushed off
And kicked and pulled;

Pushed off
And kicked and pulled;

Pushed off
And kicked and pulled;

Pushed off
And kicked and pulled
And kicked and pulled
And kicked and pulled
And kicked and pulled
And kicked and pulled
I SWAM.

And I'll never forget the feeling.

Daphne Kitching

Packing, John?

'You will need
for this school trip,'
the list read:

> 'Two pairs of shoes
> (one may be trainers)
> one anorak
> and some spare trousers
> three shirts, two jumpers
> shorts (perhaps)
> four vests
> and underpants.
> A towel and soap
> toothbrush and paste
> all to be packed
> in one small case.
>
> N.B.
> AMPLE socks.
> NO alarm clocks.
> Games (quiet).
> A few sweets
> if desired
> and
> ONE
> GOOD
> BOOK.'

'Packing, John?'

'Just starting, Mum.'

'Six cans of Coke
the same for crisps
ten chocolate bars
digestive bics.
Two packs of cards
computer game
mags and comics
(packing's a pain!)

Now for the rest.
          What's left?

Batman underpants
and caggie,
shirt, bermudas,
sweater (baggy),
pair of socks.
Never can tell –
I'll just cram in
my best hair gel.

Cor!
Humph!
(click)
Shut!'

'Finished, John?'

'Yes, Mum.'

'Don't forget the soap.
John? . . . John?

DON'T FORGET THE SOAP!'

Patricia Leighton

Year 6 Residential

We hiked a hundred miles
(Sir said five)

Got stuck in a bog
(Lucky to be alive)

Made our beds
(Though I can't imagine why)

Cooked our own food
(AAARRRGGGHHH I'm going to die)

Climbed a perilous mountain
(Well, a hill)

Nearly drowned in canoes
(Utterly brill)

Got chased by a (probably cloned)
Killer sheep

The only thing we didn't do
Was sleep.

Frances Nagle

Lost

We've lost a whole class on an outing.
They only went off for the day.
The geography master
(a hopeless disaster!)
insisted he knew the right way.

Well-armed with ten maps and an atlas,
they set off for Bilberry Tor,
down Sycamore Alley,
through Tumbleton Valley,
then back to the school.
Nothing more.

So if you should happen to see them,
please show them the way, and do hurry!
No further delays –
they've been gone seven days,
and their parents are starting to worry.

Barry Buckingham

The Mystery Walk

Tomorrow, Year 6, as part
of your week of activities,
we're going to take you all
on a mystery walk.

Where are we going, Sir?

Well, it wouldn't be a mystery
if I told you, Barry, would it?

*But my mum likes to know
where I am, Sir.*

Actually I don't know either,
I'm as much in the dark as you are.

*Oh come on, Sir, you planned it,
you must know.*

Correction, Barry, Mr Winters planned it.

*Oh well, in that case it will be a mystery.
He can't even find his way to the right classroom
and he's been here twenty years . . .*

As I was saying, or trying to say,
you will all assemble here tomorrow
at 9 o'clock.

What if it rains, Sir?

You'll get wet, Barry,
W E T, wet.

But my Mum doesn't like me getting wet, sir,
I catch cold easily,
I'll be off school . . .

Well, let us all hope for rai . . . a fine day,
all right, Barry, may I continue?

Oh yes, Sir, please do, Sir.

Make sure, Year 6, that you bring
a packed lunch . . .

Salami sandwiches. I love salami sandwiches,
don't you, Sir?
Salami sandwiches with mustard, or pickle,
pickle's nice, Sir . . .

I DON'T CARE WHAT YOU BRING, BARRY.
YOU CAN BRING A WHOLE STRING OF SALAMI
    SAUSAGES,
HALF A DOZEN WATERMELONS,
A HUNDRED ICED BUNS
AND TEN GALLONS OF FIZZY DRINK,
THEN STUFF YOURSELF SILLY . . .
NOW JUST BE QUIET AND LET ME CONTINUE.

When the coach drops you off
you'll be given an envelope
with instructions for finding your way home.

What if we don't get home before dark, Sir?
My mum . . .

I know, Barry, she doesn't like you being out after dark.

That's right, Sir.

Don't worry, Barry, we'll find you long before dark.

So you do know where we're going, Sir.
I knew it, he does know where we're going,
you can't trust teachers,
they say one thing and mean another.

Have you quite finished, Barry?

Yes, Sir.

Right, take a walk, Barry.

Now, Sir?

Right now, Barry. And, Barry . . .

Yes, Sir.

This time I do know where you're going.

Where's that, Sir?

To the Headteacher, Barry, I've had enough.

But, Sir . . . my mum doesn't like me going to the Headteacher!!!

Brian Moses

School Outing

Class Four, isn't this wonderful?
Gaze from your windows, do.
Aren't those beauteous mountains heavenly?
Just drink in that gorgeous view.

Sir, Linda Frost has fainted
Aw, Sir, I think she's dead
And Kenny Mound's throwing sandwiches round
I've got ketchup all over my head.

Oh, aren't these costumes just super?
Please notice that duchess's hat!
You can write up your notes for homework tonight,
I know you'll look forward to that.

Sir, Antoinette Toast says she's seen the ghost
Of that woman, Lady Jane Grey
And I don't know where Billy Beefcake is
But the armour is walking away.

And here in this ghastly dungeon
The prisoners were left to die.
Oh, it's all just so terribly touching
I'm afraid I'm going to cry.

Sir, Stanley Slack has put Fred on the rack
Sir, somebody's pinched your coat
Sir, Melanie Moreland's dived off the wall and
Is doing the crawl round the moat.

Well, here we are, homeward bound again –
It's been a wonderful day
I know when you meet your parents and friends
You'll have so many things to say.

Sir, what is that siren wailing for?
Sir, what's that road block ahead?
Sir, Tommy Treat is under the seat
Wearing a crown on his head.

Gareth Owen

A Sense of History

Dry were the words,
dry as the rustling page,
flatly describing extraordinary historical events;
the repeated rebellions of three princes, and
the king their father's dying rage.
The imprisoned queen was a dull figure,
silent actress on a paper stage.

But visiting the real royal castle
on a day trip from school,
metre-thick walls of cold grey stone
jarred imagination. Their senses were stimulated
to a sudden raw grasp of the reality of such rule.
Brutal spiked maces and double-edged swords
brought the youngest prince's cruel
actions frighteningly alive.
They smelled the stench of the midden,
heard squealing pigs and cackling fowl
among hovels hard by the grim defensive walls.
They saw guttering candles in draughty hidden
tower rooms, gloomy and bare, and shuddered
at the thought of being forbidden
ever to leave this damp, unhealthy place.
Ten years a captive guarded here?

Gladly they boarded the coach
for home and modern comforts,
history having momentarily come too near.

Penny Kent

The Merchant's House, Saffron Walden

The warden said this house was old.
Certainly it was rich with the scent of wood.

We laughed when the floors sloped,
And the room doors creaked,
And the pigeons made rude cooings on the roof.

But when I sat alone to write,
At the twist of the silent stair,
Deep in the threadbare tapestries,
I saw the faded people come and go,
About their common work and play,
And felt, just then, almost unsure
Who were the ghosts
That day.

Penny Dolan

Postcard From School Camp

Dear Mum and Dad,

Weather's poor, food's bad, teachers are grumpy,
instructors are mad. Cramped in tent, cold at night, no dry
clothes, boots too tight. Didn't like canoeing, hiking was
tough, all in all I've had enough.

Bye for now, <u>may</u> see you soon.
If I survive this afternoon.
Your loving son.
Charlie X X

P.S. Can I come again next year?

Richard Caley

Squirrels and Motorbikes

Today we went out of school
Down the lane
Into the spinney,
To watch squirrels.

We saw lots of grey squirrels,
Some climbing in the trees and
Looking for food on the ground.
Some still as statues.

We all did notes
And made sketches.
And asked questions.

Back in school,
We drew our squirrels.
Some sitting like silver-grey coffee pots.
Some busy paddling acorns
Into the soft green grass.
Some posing, listening with their tufty ears.
Others with feather-duster tails.

Everyone drew a squirrel picture, except –
Ahmed who drew a motorbike
But then he always does.

David Whitehead

Summer Story Time

The best thing about listening
to a story on the school field
is that you can . . .

swap places,
pull funny faces,
make daisy chains,
whisper names,
do cartwheels,
nibble secret meals,
carry teacher's chair
comb your neighbour's hair,
and, if all else fails,
listen to your teacher's tales . . . if you like!

Andrew Collett

At the End of a School Day

It is the end of a school day
    and down the long driveway
come bag-swinging, shouting children.
    Deafened, the sky winces.
        The sun gapes in surprise.

Suddenly the runners skid to a stop,
    stand still and stare
at a small hedgehog
    curled up on the tarmac
        like an old, frayed cricket ball.

A girl dumps her bag, tiptoes forward
    and gingerly, so gingerly
carries the creature
    to the safety of a shady hedge.
        Then steps back, watching.

Girl, children, sky and sun
    hold their breath.
There is a silence,
    a moment to remember
        on this warm afternoon in June.

Wes Magee

Too Hot for School

It's scorching hot. Too hot for school.
We should be floating in a pool,
darting, diving, skimming through
a paradise of watery blue.
It's criminal to keep us here.
If only we could disappear,
vanish in a puff of smoke
and splash into a pool to soak
or surf on waves on golden beaches
far from school and grouchy teachers.
Our teacher's very grouchy, she
points a finger. Yes, it's me.
'You,' she thunders, hot and red,
'have not listened to a word I've said.'
And it's quite true, I'm just not troubling.
It's far too hot, my brain is bubbling
and if they ring the home bell late,
I think I may evaporate.

Marian Swinger

Daisies

Blazing June. Dinnertime.
The whole school lazes.
Playfield and lawns
Are white with daisies.

Daisy chains! Let's make
Garlands for teachers!
It might improve
Their hideous features!

What, even for Benbow
(Who's always grim)?
Yes, Benbow, too:
Especially him!

And so it was made,
Ben's daisy ring –
An airy, fairy
Dare of a thing.

Then, greatly daring,
Liz and Ted
Crept up and looped it
Over Ben's head,
And gasped and giggled –
And turned and fled.

What then – with the whole school
Holding its breath?
Would Benbow explode?
Cause ruin? Or death?
But no; on his face
Appeared, they say,
A slight, slight smile,
That hot June day.

Eric Finney

Hot Day at the School

All day long the sun glared
as fiercely as a cross Headteacher.

Out on the brown, parched field
we trained hard for next week's Sports Day.

Hedges wilted in the heat:
teachers' cars sweltered on the tarmac.

In the distance a grenade of thunder
exploded across the glass sky.

Wes Magee

Summer Fair

No PE today – instead
we are carrying tables onto the field,
putting benches in rows,
marking a pitch for the coconut shy.

Instead of maths, there are numbers on corks –
and if it divides by five
you win a prize.
Boxes and bottles gleam in high piles,
teddy bears wink at packets of sweets.

No literacy hour, but half of Year Six
are printing bright posters,
'Admission 50p.' 'Try your luck.'
'Book bargains here.'

History hovers about the white elephants,
black and white postcards with pictures of trams,
a tortoiseshell hairslide, enormous telephone,
three yellow cups with polkadot saucers.

There are no school dinners in the canteen,
but mountains of cakes, pastel iced,
jewelled with silver balls and smarties.

Instead of the science topic
there are trays in the corner
full of marigold suns, white bursts of alyssum,
blue lobelia, velvet pansies.

Nobody's thinking of lessons –
even Miss Sefton's smiling,
saying she doesn't think it will rain.

Why can't we do this every week?

Alison Chisholm

School Report

Mum, before you read that letter,
yes, I know I could do better.
Yes, I know I make a noise
and fight with all the other boys;
and in case there's any mention
that I never pay attention,
yes, I know I must be good
when the teacher says I should.
And I know I shouldn't play
till I've put my books away,
and I shouldn't say that word
that the teacher overheard.
I must finish all my writing
when the field looks so inviting,
and my sums must be complete
before I try to leave my seat.
So please, Mum, when you start to read
my report, you really need
to remember that I'll try
working harder, and that's why . . .

What's that, Mum? It's not so bad?
I'm really quite a clever lad?
Phew, that's fine. Well, just ignore
all the things I said before.

Alison Chisholm

Parents' Evening

So you are Matthew's mother
Then you must be his dad?
I'm so very pleased to meet you,
I'm extremely glad.
He's such a gifted pupil,
And such a little dear,
There's been a vast improvement
In all his work this year.
His writing is exceptional,
So beautifully neat,
His spelling quite incredible,
His poetry a treat.
His number work is flawless
And his painting so inspired.
He's interested and lively,
And he's never ever tired.
He's amazingly athletic,
And excels in every sport.
Your Matty is the brightest child
That I have ever taught.
I should say he's gifted –
He comes top in every test.
In fact in every single subject
Your Matthew is the best!
I must say Mr and Mrs Flynn,
You're fortunate to have a child like him.
Pardon?
Oh! You're not Matthew's father,
Then you can't be his mum.
You say I've got the names mixed up.

Oh dear! What have I done?
Well, I'm very, very sorry.
So your child's Matthew Brown.
Well, before I tell you about your son
You had better both sit down!

Gervase Phinn

And I'm at Home While
They're at School

Mum and Dad have read my report
and it's okay . . .
not brilliant, but it's okay.
They haven't shouted at me or anything
so I've not been too worried . . . until tonight.

Now that it's Parents' Evening
And I'm at home while they're at school
I'm starting to worry, a bit.
I know I've done okay
but I can't help being nervous.

What if the teachers get me mixed up?
Or what about that one time when I got detention for
    talking?
What if my marks were wrong and there's been a mis-
    take?
Will the teachers be nice . . . or not?

And I'm at home while they're at school,
looking at the living room window.
And I'm at home while they're at school
watching for the headlights to flash then dim.
And I'm at home while they're at school
listening for the car doors.
And I'm at home while they're at school
waiting for the gravel to crunch.
And I'm at home while they're at school

wondering whether the front door will slam angrily
or click closed quietly.

While they're at school I'm at home
Worrying.

Paul Cookson

Joint Champions

Jamie's not much good at running
Jodie can't throw very far
Jamie's useless at the sack race
Jodie *hates* the high jump bar
Jamie's spoon is always eggless
Jodie's clothes race is a mess

When it comes to the 'three-legged'
– well, just guess!

Jamie's long jump's on the short side
Jodie's feet don't reach the sand
Jamie's scoreless at the goal kicks
Jodie's skipping's far from grand

But they both can't wait for Sports Day
That's the day they really shine

Jamie ————————————————————— Jodie

Top tape holders
At the winning line!

Patricia Leighton

Sports Day!

Now you mustn't worry
it won't be like last year,
this time I'm prepared
even got all the gear!

I know last Sports Day
there was a bit of an alarm
but I couldn't help falling
and breaking my arm!

Now you must understand
the family pride is at stake
but this time – no slip-up,
trip-up or silly mistake.

Yes, I've done all the sweating,
I've *even* lost weight
just stand back and watch me
as I take-off – accelerate.

So off to the finish,
and look out for the first place,
for it's time for me to take part
in the annual Father's Race!

Ian Souter

Junior School Sports

Sports Day's over.
It's four o'clock.
The mats have all been stacked away,
the benches and the chairs
all cleared away,
the mums and dads and little kids
have all gone home for tea.

There's just a handful of us
Sixth Years stayed behind
to help collect up all the bean-bags,
hoops and balls,

Sports Day's over.
But what a great day!
I won the rounders ball,
a throw of 40 metres – beat the record!
The one thing, maybe the only thing,
I'm really good at.
This has been the best day of my life.

The last week
of the last term
of the Fourth Year.
Tomorrow is the very last day

and I don't want today to end
I want to stretch this afternoon out
like a rubber band, I want
this afternoon to last
for ever.

Daft!
I know it can't.
I've seen all year how
everything's too small,
how I've outgrown it all –

the chairs too low,
the corridors too narrow,
the climbing ropes too easy,
the playground and the hall too cramped.

Sports Day's over
and that's that.
At my feet
the last wire crate of rounders balls,
the last thing
waiting to be put away.

Next year
It'll all be different.
I'll be a First Year then,
just a little kid again.
I won't be best any anything next year!

Go on, girl –
one last throw?

A short run –
           back foot
                     front foot – Hurl!

Watch it soar –
20 – 30 – 40 metres . . . Go on! Go on!
50 – 60 . . . Don't stop! Don't ever stop!
See the white ball
arc across the clear blue sky –

'**Julie!** I'm surprised at you!
This isn't the time to
mess about.
Go and get it
– **now!**'

'Yes, Miss. Sorry, Miss,
don't worry, Miss,
It won't happen again –'

Mick Gowar

It's Not What I'm Used To

I don't want to go to Juniors . . .

The chairs are too big.
I like my chair small, so I fit
Exactly
And my knees go
Just so
Under the table.

And that's another thing –
The tables are too big.
I like my table to be
Right
For me
So my workbook opens
Properly.
And my pencil lies in the space at the top
The way my thin cat stretches into a long line
On the hearth at home.

Pencils – there's another other thing.
Another problem.
Up in Juniors they use pens and ink.
I shall really have to think

About ink.

Jan Dean

Last Day

This class was special.

No one was particularly clever,
Particularly naughty,
Particularly messy,
Particularly anything.

Nothing miraculous happened,
Nothing stunning,
Or funny, or frightening, or strange.

Each day was much like another
As the year crept softly by,
Leaving its ordinary debris
Of drawings and stories
And small successes
And unremarkable memories.

Yet something hung between us,
Something that glittered like chalk dust
On a sunny day.

It was nothing you could touch,
Or capture,
Or exactly define,
But when I see the scattered offerings
Left on my desk –
A necklace of shells,
A giant pot of talcum
Smelling of yesterday,

A limp bunch of yellow flowers,
A crumpled card
Signed with love –
I can hardly bear
To walk away.

This class was special.

Clare Bevan

Last Assembly

At our last assembly
some children cried
and others blew their noses
pretending not to cry.
At our last assembly
Mrs Bailey got some flowers and a clap
because she was leaving
             – to have a baby . . .
and Mr Miles got a clap
because he was leaving
but not having a baby.
At our last assembly
Mrs Wiseman said it was
a sad day
and a happy day
and didn't get anything.
Mr Miles got teacher of the year award
but not a clap
because no one liked him.
At our last assembly we
stood for the last time
to sing the school hymn
but someone had put a football sock
in the piano
so we didn't.
At our last assembly
I got
my last detention.

Peter Dixon

Nearly

Half an hour to go
Each tick of the clock
Kicks the second hand
Closer to home time.

Sunlight streams
Down half-open windows,
Halfway home
Our thoughts scatter.

To perfect beaches in the sun
Swimming pools and aeroplanes
Busy cities far away
Country lanes, long green hills.
Endless hours of nothing.

Ten minutes to go
We hold our breath
The classroom clock
Clears its throat.

Crams more minutes
In its tick-tock mouth
Swallows hard,
Thirty seconds left.

David Harmer

Tit for Tat

I hate Sir
and Sir hates me.

Yesterday
we had to write
about our favourite
memories of this school
and I said

Mine'll be when I leave next Wednesday

and Sir said
Well, Ricki.
I'm glad you and I
have at least
one thing
in common.

Fred Sedgwick

Transfer Haiku

Who will build the bridge
From one school to the other?
Will I be alone?

John Kitching

Summer Holidays

On the First Day of the Summer Holidays

Lie in bed late
      lounging and lolling about
Eat eggs and bacon
      for breakfast at eleven

Sprawl on the lawn
      with a long glass of lemonade
And eat salad and seafood
      Travel the town T-shirted

Greeting mates
      grinning with freedom Bowl
Bash those bails down
      Belt a leather ball

Bouncing to the boundary bounce bounce
      Bring
A take-away home
      parathas and popadums

Talk about treats
      sunlight through trees and sand
Sleep in deep silence between sheets
      Dream

Fred Sedgwick

Where is Everybody?

Here we are, two weeks into the summer holidays,
and there's no one around. It's not
like Alasdair who went to Loch Ard
or Cafy who went to Iran
and never came back. It's not
even like Ola who went to Bearsden
or Emma who changed schools
and were hardly seen again.
It's not even like Cassy whose mum's
full of twins and moving house.
I can understand them. It's life.
People move.
But this is strange – there's
no one. I go to the supermarket, to the park,
and there's no one I even know. I ring their bells,
I ring them up – no one answers. They can't
all be away. It's as if they'd all gone
on holiday together, to a party without inviting me.
I play with this and that, I watch telly, read comics,
sometimes go swimming or get taken places.
I even play with toddlers. I go to the gardens,
kick a ball, hide in trees.
But there's a big hole inside me. I keep
expecting my friends to jump from the bushes
shouting surprise. I wonder
who'll be there when school starts again.
Will I be in a class of one?

Dave Calder

Going to Secondary
(for Faith)

The summer holidays are almost over.
Everyone's been on holiday
and come back sun-tanned.
Children sleep late then play all day.

Each early morning is misty and chilled,
as if the season has become fed up with
the same old hot days and wants a change.

In just four days, time I shall be going
to secondary school.
I have never been as excited as this!

My new uniform hangs in the wardrobe
and every now and again, I wander upstairs
pretending I'm going to read a book or something,
but really I just want to look at my new uniform.

I run my fingers across the yellow
diagonal stripes on my black tie,
or try on my black jacket
(it's just a little too long in the sleeves,
but my mum says it's got to last a few years).
I am really looking forward to putting it on
and walking with my friends to secondary school
in the cool morning sunshine.

My friends! Of course!
I can't wait to see my friends
in *their* uniforms! No more little
blue jumpers like we wore in primary!
No more boring clothes and shoes with buckles,
we're going to wear slip-ons and the latest fashions.

Only four days to go and I'll be
at secondary school. I feel like the
whole world is hurtling and spinning
and zooming and changing –
and me, little me, I'm right in the middle of it!

What if I get lost in that huge school?
It's vast and maze-like with hundreds
of corridors and classes.
What if I'm late on the very first day – oh no!

Mum says we'll go into town on Monday morning
and get my shoes, and then that's it –
I'll be ready!
(What if they don't have my size?)

I'm so excited and then again,
I'm so nervous and anxious!
Only four more days,
four more days and I'll be
at secondary school.

Say goodbye to childhood for me.

John Rice

Back to School Blues

Late August,
The miserable countdown starts,
Millions of kids
With lead in their hearts.
In Woolies' window: rubbers, rulers,
Geometry sets,
And a BACK TO SCHOOL sign –
I mean, who forgets?
In the clothes shops
Ghastly models of kids with
New satchels and blazers and shoes:
Enough to give anybody
Those Back to School Blues.

And Auntie Nell from Liverpool,
Who's down with us for a visit,
Smiles and says, 'So it's back to school
On Wednesday for you, is it?
I only wish I'd got the chance
Of my schooldays over again . . .
Happiest days of my life they were –
Though I didn't realize it then . . . '
And she rabbits on like that,
Just twisting away at the screws;
She's forgotten about
The Back to School Blues.

And six and a half long weeks
Have melted away like ice cream:
That Costa Brava fortnight's
Vanished like a dream.
And Dad says, 'Look, this term
At school, could you try and do
A bit better?
For a start you could learn to spell
And write a decent letter.
    And just keep away from that Hazel Stephens –
She's total bad news . . . '
Any wonder that I've got
Those Back to School Blues?

Eric Finney

Change

The summer
still hangs
heavy and sweet
with sunlight
as it did last year.

The autumn
still comes
showering gold and crimson
as it did last year.

The winter
still stings
clean and cold and white
as it did last year.

The spring
still comes
like a whisper in the dark night.

It is only I
who have changed.

Charlotte Zolotow

Acknowledgements

The publishers would like to thank the following for permission to reprint the selections in this book:

Allan Ahlberg, 'Supply Teacher' from *Please Mrs Butler* by Allan Ahlberg, Kestrel, 1983. Copyright © Allan Ahlberg 1983. Reprinted by permission of Penguin Books.
Ann Bonner, 'February 14th' from *Let's Celebrate*, edited by John Foster, OUP, 1989.
Author and John Johnsons authors' agent – Max Fatchen for 'Look Out'.
'Netball' from *School Poems*, edited by Jennifer Curry, Scholastic, 1999.
Richard Caley, 'Postcard From School Camp' from *Bats, Balls and Balderdash*, Durrington Press Ltd, 1998.
Jennifer Curry, 'Winter Playground' from *Down Our Street* by Jennifer and Graeme Curry, Methuen.
David Higham Associates for: 'Prince Rama Comes to Longsight' by John Cunliffe and 'School Bell' by Eleanor Farjeon, from *Blackbird has Spoken*, Macmillan Children's Books.
Gwen Dunn, 'I Went Back', from *Stories and Rhymes*, BBC.
Eric Finney, 'Back to School Blues', first published in *Another Third Poetry Book*, edited by John Foster, OUP, 1988.
John Foster, 'The Test' from *Making Waves*, OUP, 1997. Reprinted by permission of the author.
Chrissie Gittins, 'Tuup the Story-Teller' from *The Listening Station*, Dagger Press, 1998,
David Harmer, 'Exams' from *School's Out*, edited by John Foster, OUP.
Wes Magee, 'Grey Squirrel' from *Morning Break and Other Poems*, Cambridge University Press, 1989. 'Disco Night' from *The Boneyard Rap and Other Poems*, Hodder Wayland, 2000.
Brian Moses, 'Windy Playground', first published in *Knock Down Ginger and Other Poems*, Cambridge University Press, 1994. 'Day Closure' from *The Secret Lives of Teachers*, Macmillan Children's Books, 1996.
Judith Nicholls, 'School Visit' from *Dragonsfire*, Faber and Faber, 1990. Reprinted by permission of the author.
Gareth Owen, 'School Outing' from *Gareth Owen: Collected Poems*, Macmillan Children's Books, 2000.
PFD for extract from 'First Day at School' © Roger McGough, reprinted by permission of PFD on behalf of Roger McGough.